I Choose The Rhymes

Colin B Osborn

William Cornelius Harris Publishing

In collaboration
with
London Poetry Books

ISBN 978-1-911232-60-5

William Young

34 Birchwood Close, Bordesley Road SM4 5NH

London Poetry Books

Dedications

I would like to thank Vera Howard for the wonderful cover illustration.

Thanks also to Redeeming Features, Lee and Loz for their continuing inspiration, encouragement and collaboration. James and Sara for having invited me to write a poem for their wedding. Sidney for being a largely indifferent but consistent listener.

All the many poets, oddballs, artists, musicians and misfits I have met over the last few years who continue to be supportive and pursue their artistic intentions.

I dedicate this book to the memory of my Dad, Armin.

Contents

What If Aristotle Had Been An Axolotl

What if Aristotle had been an Axolotl, would his synthesis of
Disciplines have gone ahead full throttle?
What if he were a smiling 'walking fish' with protruding frontal
Wattle, known less for the stance of his Platonic rebuttal and more
For his courtly mating dance and charming little scuttle?
Would he still have gathered fellow thinkers fired up by a shuffle
Across the floors of the lyceum as they flexed their mental muscle?

Would De Anima,Organon, Nicomachean Ethics have never come
About to guide peripatetics in formation of their logic and ancient
Analytics, so beloved by the canon of philosophising critics?
What if when we utilise the term Aristotelian, we meant neotenic
Creatures who can lose and grow a tail again?
Caught between the land and a lifestyle more aquatic, would the
Impact of his musings have been nearly so dramatic?

What if Anaximander had been a fire Salamander?
Would he still have had a gander at the stars and think,
Oh man the
Current classification deserves more cogitation, here's some
Further explanation
Of the planetary formations.
Or would naming constellations display amphibious limitations?
Given that their conversation rarely helps elucidation, would
Ectothermic inclinations match mammalian fixations?
Perhaps talk at cross stations would impede such revelations.

Knowing he suggested men started out as fish, would the intellect
Invested have dismissed this impish twist?
Or perhaps reversed the story, first came man and then John
Dory. Would he have claimed he saw the missing causal link, that
as Humans we began before returning to the drink.
Would his vibrant colouration have distracted concentration, or his
Ideas seem so pithy with the threat of toxi-city?

Now imagine Xenophon had been a chameleon. Though the
Scansion is slightly wrong we can still string this along.
Could chameleonic condition have engendered erudition to this
Talented tactician known for his martial wisdom?
For its subterfuge most suited to bring its mission to fruition.
Its aim is to camouflage and erase traces, not put soldiers through
Their paces and commit tactics to pages to be looked at through
The ages.

Would the germ of Anabasis have remained in larval stasis and not
Received its status In Quintillian's praises?
Would this honey tongued polymath have still embarked upon the
Path that described the might of Sparta's wrath and made Al the
Great just for a laugh seize Babylon within his grasp?
Would he merely be content to clasp passing bugs and not to ask,
Why don't I finish the great task embarked on by Thucydides in
Writing battle histories?

What if Euclid of Megara had been a Tuatara?
Would his didactic conventions never get another mention?
Would the blending between notions Eleatic and Socratic and the
Declaration, *All is good*, been nearly as emphatic?

Though some scholars were confused and thought he wrote on
Mathematics,
No rhyming reptile fits his namesake,
So he's not in these schematics.

But had our chosen Euclid been the last rhynchocephalian still
Going, would Megarian instruction have got a proper showing?
As Tuataras are of Polynesian extraction in the Western corpus his
Teachings may not have found much traction.
Would his pitch that in a pinch Eristic fixes were a cinch, just have
Been nixed without a hint for future stoics to half inch?
The unfortunate position of his scholastic omission, only serving to
Worsen the conditions for logicians.

If these pontificators were all reptile or amphibian, would their
cogency of thought have been merely quotidian?
Would the light their theories shone have been altogether more
Obsidian and their impact diminished across globalised meridians?
Maybe reptilian theory would be worth considering, but their output
Up to now has regrettably been piddling.
If the outlook for such works is probably poor to middling, it might
Be because they lack the means to begin scribbling.
There may just be a genius who's yet to get exposure lurking in the
Corner of the reptile house enclosure.

Middle Of Lidl

Our eyes locked across the aisle
In the middle of Lidl.
You had your teeth in
So there was minimal dribble.
I was busily picking a suitable pickle,
I'm typically dill
But that day I felt fickle.
Thought fuck it,
I may as well live a little.
I tried a quick quip
And you let out a giggle.

I opted for cornichons
You were noncommittal,
Said 'They're alright I guess'
But in your tone was dismissal.

Then with slickly glib precision
You pithily listed
The particulars
Of your resistant position.
Icily diminishing their
Miniature stature
As insufficient
To warrant inclusion
In your gherkin provision.

I listened politely
But still felt their excision
Didn't fit in with my
Incipient vision.
Clearly in our respective
Preservative prisms
There were tangible schisms.

I nipped in the bud
Any further addition
To your fervent derision
Of my dining decision.
In this bid for concision
I sensed the elision
Of more stirred up opinion
On the brined goods dominion.

Pickle picked, I switched
To thinking which
Nibbly bits would fit
Within my cats remit.
I'd imagined we'd split
But quickly twigged
This inquisitive dig
Into our twin shopping lists
Was not yet nixed.

Your intimation implicit,
As I laid visuals on the biscuits,
Was that I'd wildly mispicked
And you were surprised I would risk this
Imposition on any whiskered
Accomplice.

I declined to divine why
This brand might make you whine.
Fingers drilling paradiddle
Rhythms whilst gripping the kibble,
I invited enlightening insight
On your particular riddle.

I figured you kidded
When you wistfully whispered
You were a biblical literalist
With an interest in wizards.

How to reconcile scriptural syllables
With wizardly rituals
Incited ideation that trips and pills
Were your habitual victuals.
Did this dissonant thinking
Signify intemperate drinking?

Indeed I wished I was sinking suds
While your blinkered disquisition
On the human condition
Pinpointed bigotry
With zero contrition.

Clearly no rhetorician,
Nor linguistic magician
Garden shed level intellect
Met with prejudicial
Suppositions.
I regretted my inauspicious
Initiation of discursive inquisition.

So now when out shopping
I've fully learnt my lesson,
I'll be focused where I look
A supermarket Luc Besson.
I'll Keep my gaze on the displays
And then firmly press on
To the specific produce I require,
So such scenes won't once more transpire

Where store Based bores
Who converse without pause
Advocate for causes flawed
In a sordid onslaught of thoughts
They've only half explored.
Now if I'm tempted by some flippant aside
I'll think of the last time I tried
And I'll recall the squall of rhetorically derivative drivel
I was subjected to, in the Middle of Lidl.

Ode To Dubious Eateries

This rhyme recalls
The down at heel diners,
And filthy food halls,
The risible bistros
With paint peeling walls,
The lugubrious eateries,
Germ ridden gaffs,
The dubious restaurants
And grime ravaged cafs.

The places so greasy
You could lube up a nun,
With eggs over queasy
And steaks over done.
Where the hygiene is lacking
Lax standards apply,
The coffees abysmal,
The calories high.

The bangers are flaccid
And the mystery pie
Is served with a wink
And unsavoury grin,
A pastry roulette
That may just do you in.
To the drumsticks
Still bloodied
Beneath breaded skin,

The vinegary condiments
Sour and thin,
The disgustingly gut busting
Layers of spread,
Slathered on slabs
Of pappy white bread.

To the mystery fish
That's ostensibly cod,
The flavourless gravy
That's colour is odd,
To the slurry of curries
That offend the gut,
The leathery burgers
Dispensed from a hut.
To the dodgy chinese
With glutinous sauce
And enough msg
For a year in each course.

To the shocking salt levels
And fearsome meat sweats,
All served with a side
Of dyspeptic regret.
A paean to places
In forgotten towns,
Whose greatest achievement's
Not being shut down.
To the ramshackle joints
With washed out interiors,
Who dispense complimentary

Bouts of listeria.
Though it's true these places
May not be much fun
I've dined in and enjoyed
The food from each one.

Gainful Employment

Putting in the hard graft,
Lifting and shifting,
Some will craft
While others are grifting.
Some may accuse you of drifting
Because your story
Doesn't fit their scripting.
They might even launch a diatribe
Against your lack of nine to five,
Tell you that to stay alive
You must grind and scrimp and strive.
Get a job, gainful employment,
Worry not about enjoyment,
Here's some possible deployments:

Morticians spend all day with stiffs,
So do porn stars if you catch my drift,
Seismologists monitor rifts,
Bellhops pass the time in lifts.
One role for Egyptologists
Is digging into hieroglyphs.
Your stuff is taken by bailiffs,
Search and rescue go up cliffs,
Marriage counsellors placate tiffs,
Rockstars play their biggest riffs.
Barbers deals with trims and quiffs,
Rhinoplasticians that which sniffs,
Perfumiers concoct nice whiffs,

Popes sit supreme betwixt pontiffs.
Philosophers ponder what ifs,
Someone's paid to roll
Snoop Dogg's spliffs.
Darth Vader he served the Sith,
Prince made music named as a glyph.

Comedians they deal in quips,
Dominatrices with whips,
Sailors ply their trade on ships,
Dealers dispense dope and trips.
Gymnasts they get paid for flips,
Botox clinicians filling lips,
Fixers try to lessen blips,
Mixologists invite your sips.
Bed sellers promise good kips,
Chicken shops flog wings and strips,
Bra makers aim for well housed nips,
Bloods gangbang and fight with Crips.
Tailors they attend to rips,
Tech bros trade in microchips,
Agony aunts offer tips,
Tree surgeons give branches clips,
Plumbers solve unwanted drips.

Pugilists utilise fists,
Watchmakers they adorn wrists,
Paparazzi badger the A-list,
Matchmakers engineer trysts.
Dr Pimple popper, she drains cysts,
Police arrest those who resist,

P.A.s ensure meetings aren't missed.
Urologists they deal with with piss,
Ontologists that which exists.

This is no comprehensive list
But by now you must get the gist.
No matter how much they insist
You're not tied down, you can resist,
The notion you must stick, not twist.
It's your life do as you wish,
Cos there's no second chance at this!

I Choose The Rhymes

I thought we might have made it
It seems that I was wrong
I thought we were in chorus
But I'm singing my own song

I'd have liked to know what happened
Had we stuck upon our trail
But I now know that's not to be
All these ideas are curtailed

In the end you must be honest
Both to others and yourself
There's no point in pretending
It will skew your mental health

So I'll state it boldly
Though with you it doesn't chime
I choose the life in pursuit of the rhyme

I can't offer you a mortgage
I can't promise you a house
I've no interest in investments
Or life as trad married spouse

I don't want quiet nights in
Or at least not as the norm
I don't want cars or kids
Or a neatly tended lawn

I want words shared round a fire
I want similes well wrought
I want the feeling that's inspired
When a grain of truth is caught
Wrapped within a poem
Printed on the page
Delivered by a speaker
Standing on the stage

I want the mad jaunts
And the travelling chats
The joyful spirit that haunts
Those who write sing and rap

I want the rhythm the metre
The visions, the craft
The high that you get
When you finish a draft

I want the wisdom the pathos
The insight the wit
The smut the absurdity
The off kilter skit
The surprise and the wonder
The beauty in words

The new ways of phrasing
That you've never heard
The pain the desire
The anger the strife

The asides and addendums
To this mess we call life

So I guess then at this juncture
We must say farewell
I sincerely hope you find
That which rings your bell

But should you pose the question
Even if a thousand times
Each and every answer will be
I choose the rhymes

Speech Therapy

See I used to be tongue tied,
A small slip of superfluous tissue
Connecting tongue to mouth
Caused a locution issue.
Whereby over certain words I'd stumble,
A jumble of pronunciations duly fumbled.

It was the lingual frenulum
To use the correct description,
Was held by excess flesh
That interfered with my diction.
By this addition unneeded
Vocalising was impeded,
And if my verbals were heeded
Improper wordage proceeded.

My v's were b's,
While t's and d's were teased
Into conceits that cleaved
Far from the Queens received.

Indeed, were my speech perceived
It'd read like a mediaeval screed,
Conceived pre-consonantal
Conventions having been decreed.
But a minor procedure

My tongue's movement freed.

They cut back that flap
Causing the curb
On my discursive intentions,
And to perturb
Further disturbance
Of the words that I'd mention
It was decided I be guided
By therapeutic attention.

Any mangled syntax that remained intact
Would be put back on track,
And I'd soon redact
All the traces of my former Ankyloglossia,
If I studiously pursued
The route supplied in the dossier.

Through language exercises
And correct declarations,
I'd divest myself completely
Of suspect formulations,
When engaging in the process
Of polite conversation.
Still make faux pas's sure,
But not through enunciation

I took to heart the injunction,
That linguistic function
Required proper application
To avoid the compunction

Awoken when conversants
Deemed my words to be minced.
I Formed an aversion to the thought
My meaning wasn't distinct.

Similarly piqued an interest
In the way that words sync
With the nebulous array
Of random things that we think.
Still puzzling that one,
Both in my head and in ink.

But I digress,
My ideas weren't yet that progressive;
Can I really attest to
Having pensively tested
The cybernetics of phonetics?
Well I was only 5,
So my pondering of articulable concepts
Would have been most precocious in its onset.

But lexicographically speaking,
An interest was creeping
In the manner by which words
Could be the salve I was seeking.

How cognisant I was of morphological cogs,
I couldn't say, but knew the concept of my competence was
Contained within the context of how chat came across.
Not to say I only counted up in profit and loss,
But fixation on oration gave a comforting gloss,

To things over which at that age I could never be boss.

Then growing older I'd behold how old conjectural plots
Could be resold as we were told the leopard now had new spots.
Saw how connections concocted by honey tongued convocants,
Could be conned and contorted just to realise their wants.

Or conversely how conversationalists of nobler intent
Could corral a camaraderie through words wisely spent,
With winning intimations and positive takes
Soothing troubled folk to move on from mistakes.

Consideration of the spoken would continue to grow,
Contemplation been awoken by that course long ago,
Of words potential power it had left me convinced,
The value of the speech act thoroughly evinced
And I've been wordily talking bollocks ever since.

Our Blessed Virgin

Should the lemon become a sign of saccharinity
The King's elocution marked by patavinity
Da Vinci's fame based upon asininity
Trump adopt a modest clandestinity
Agoraphobes advocate for peregrinity
Andrew Tate be found to praise femininity
The dead sea become devoid of salinity
The rabbinical council renounce all divinity
Richard Dawkins announce his new faith in the trinity
Rangers and Celtic play with equanimity
Joan of Arc stand accused of pusillanimity
Katie Hopkins project a tone of sanguinity
Custer become renowned for supinity
Should all reasoned deduction quit the vicinity
One thing we can rely on
Is Anne Widdicombe's virginity

Panopticonundrum

Of concepts that cast shadows long
There's quite a few among the throng,
The collected works of Cheech and Chong
The finer points of Falun Gong,
The Archetypes set out by Jung,
Why Sisquo fetishized the thong,
The exact nature of friendship
Between Tiny Planets Bing and Bong.
But within this poem we'll go on
To ponder the panopticon.

Can this Benthamite structure
Still prove instructive?
Or is the motif no longer productive,
A construct redundant and largely reductive.
Is it only an image remaining seductive
For incurably eager armchair Foucauldians
Who gaspingly harp about its vaunted podium?

Is this a stance to be met with opprobrium
Or for intellects incontinent conceptual imodium?
The fact that this piece has even been written
May hint just a little at my supposition.

So Where lies the significance
Of this visage of omniscience?
First a physical solution
To subdue institutions

And realise the execution
Of a smoother retribution.
Meant to curb the constitution
Of those aimed at dissolution,
With the threat of being watched
A fact of the prosecution
That ensured the imminution
Of attempts at revolution.

Would the construction concentric
Feigning constant attention
Diminish recidivist criminal tension?
Did Bentham intend his brother's invention
To bend the conventions, not just of detention?
Are the utilitarian ends that he mentioned served by the concepts
Creeping extension into the realm of the self's reinvention?

Where,

Beyond the cylindrical structure as built,
The Scintilla of cynical systems instilled
Sees sly cosseted censure infect one's own will.
As dissident missives are silently stilled,
Dismiss all Illicit intentions or thrills.
Vicissitudes fissipate governed until
Disintegrative apparatus are nil,
Internalised mechanisms have their fill.

You've paid at the entrance, you've swallowed your pills,
You've made your confessions, confronted your ills.
You've listed transgressions

You've mopped up your spills.

The vertiginous scope of surveillance instils
The paranoid vision militantly drilled.
Which solidifies cyclical scenes that cavil
With any reflections now neatly distilled
Into miniature sessions of crippling guilt.

In time you won't wonder as you become skilled
In clipping the wings of dissent and its ilk.
Belittling difference implicitly kills
The resistant impetus being fulfilled.

Diminishing quizzical quibbles you shill
For the quickening censure of keyboard and quill.
Unwittingly tending the systems tendrils,
Extending the pretence, its grist for the mill.
But the benefits never quite seem to be real.
Deficit grows correlative to the zeal
With which you impress the strength of appeal.

What fragments of self do we take as concealed,
And what the performance that's only revealed
In light of the stare of the imagined gaze,
The peepers that creep in unknowable haze.

Are we all Ariadnes in search of a maze,
Or just scrambling mannequins grasping for ways
To obtain the unreachable through our displays?

Perhaps we're players in perceptible scenes,

The fleshly extension of portable screens.
Descrying designs of inscrutable means
Whilst mindlessly scrolling patrolling the reams
Of pornography cat pictures and memes.
As data is mined and every click noted
And ratings assigned approved and upvoted.

We traverse always viewed
In this gamified life,
Validate being seen by acquiring likes.
Almost none are immune
To the dopamine spikes
Of what we perceive
To be positive sight.

But what of attrition
The strife and perdition
That shadowy side
Of the human condition?
Anonymity grants
An implicit permission
To savagely dismiss
Another's position.
Or by the same token
To glorify what
Will always ineluctably
Be what we're not.

In our aspirant fashions
We sell ourselves short
All our info, coordinates

Ripe to be bought.
As targeted ads
And consumerist fads
Purport to dispel
What is making us sad

The disorderly courting
Of Hollow appeal
Warps ordinary stories
To imagined ideals.

Do we see in ourselves
An implied evanescence
If we fail in the recording
Of all possible progressions?

Is the deliquescence of the personal
Into a public presence
A force for self invention
Or another veiled suppression?
Which coalesces with obsession
For curation of impressions
That express a professed message
That's fallacious in its essence.

Is all the pomp and puff indicative
Of substanceless excrescence
Or the litmus test for zest
And a life lived in effervescence?

Will Humanity's concrescence

With technologies accessions
Offer hope and reviviscence,
Or just further our depressions?

Perhaps it's too imponderably nebulous to see
And Jez and Michel cannot tell us
What they think might be.
Any hot take on the optics
May prove myopic it is true.
But as you ogle all proposals
Remember nothing's out of view.

E.A. Endoskeletal Anonymous

I’m done with this normcore skeleton
Bored of these same old bones
From mandible to metatarsal
All elicit nothing but groans

This musculoskeletal assortment
Is a system outdated in mode
I suggest a new means of comportment
For this meatsack corporeal load

Overthrow ossified assumptions
Liberate all your viscera too
Too long has vertebral presumption
Dictated the things we can do

Yes skin is a remarkable feature
How it rips and reknits and holds in
But the claws of most predatory creatures
Demonstrate that it's really too thin

Swap those biceps for durable chitin
Hardwearing elastic and tough
Though some may not find it inviting
The trend will catch on soon enough

Renounce axial and appendicular
Too long they’ve been calling the shots
Once you find a new form that will click with ya

All those old joints you won't miss a jot

Carcinised morphological process
Proves there's some precedent set
In the new permutations of varied crustaceans
Crablike form is the biggest hit yet

If evolution says fab, what's better than crab
Who are we to dispute nature's arc
As those doubts you dispel while you work on that shell,
Pretty soon you'll discard of that snark

Of course there's plenty of viable pathways
You could take as you metamorphose
You're not stuck twixt a rock and a hard place
Here's some options I'd like to propose

Once you're post spinal deletion
Calcareous accretion
Could be the next step in your plans
All manner of snails go about their travails
Clad in shells as do aquatic clams

If with strictly calcite you've got a gripe
Aragonite might be more your type
Or perhaps all conchology is unappealing
And it's spiders and bees whose swag you are feeling

Internal arachnoid hydraulics
May well make you frolic
And each new breath seem a miracle

Taken in through a spiracle

There's an entomological plethora
Of external protective matter
And if I had been somewhat cleverer
Then doubtless objections would shatter

And If you find it too hard
To fully discard
Of your current construction
But still seek disruption
You could opt for both forms
In your body reborn

There is some potential to prevaricate
Why not channel the pangolin's
Protective plates?
Armadillos and turtles also hedge their bets
With the way their physical structure protects
But in the opinion of zoologists and of vets
They're not truly in the exoskeletal set

But what's taxonomical accuracy
When there's so much we'll have to unlearn to be free
Ontological quandaries may well arise
When undertaking this novel enterprise
What will it mean to debone human thinking?
A new set of values will take time to sink in

Such as Having a body that's ready for beaches
No longer implying great abs

It’s now fresh carapace
Rather than well toned ass
That’ll make the beachgoers keep tabs

Chiropractors will call you unruly
Belittle your new chosen form
But I wouldn’t worry unduly
Disregard their unwarranted scorn

Now listen they’ll say
With a look of dismay
And imperious wave of the hand
Your ideas are cute
But they fail to compute
Going boneless it simply won’t stand

Of course big orthopaedics
Insists that you need it
Their training you’d seem to redact
And an osteopath
Would declare it a gaff
All such notions seek to counteract

But there’s legs in the concept
When considered in context
Albeit of femur denuded
Galileo was once denounced as a dunce
So of course they will say you’re deluded

But if its a viable mode for changing decapoda
Then why not explode what we purport to know

Here we'll start to corrode the tired notional coda
That when physiological questions are posed
The spine is the logical argument closer
Yes, there's more to be done than we might have supposed
Let's decode how to go down this untrodden road
To the new motherlode of bodily modifications
A world of evolutionary variations

So join the movement.
And we'll make no concession
Bring an end to the era of
Endoskeletal oppression

Your Love Was Like A Wetherspoons Carpet

Your love was like a Wetherspoons carpet
Unique to a particular space
And just like those pub rugs in question
Your prettiness covered the trace
Of grime and emotional spillage
A multitude hidden within
A sticky dissimulative effort
To conceal any number of sins
The patterns at first were appealing
Seemed graceful and fresh to the eye
But they couldn't stop you revealing
The nature you'd tried to deny
Well trodden and bitter sodden
Strewn with a detrital mess
Like the Jacobites crushed at Culloden
You laid waste to the love you'd profess
Yes your love was like a Wetherspoons carpet
On contact a lot less alluring
Ok when considered at distance
But up close simply not worth enduring
Like a wetherspoons carpet your love was
Though there's one major difference it's true
I'd feel bad spilling drinks on their threadwork
But I can't say the same about you

Hobbes on Hinge

Solitary, poor, nasty, brutish and short.
No it's not my tinder bio
But life, so Hobbes thought.

Poem for James and Sara

As you stand on the cusp of matrimonial endeavour
I've envisioned a few settings you may embark on together
Be it blissful azure skies or thunderstorms you weather
That's the last pathetic fallacy I'll use for now, however
I'll profess to no great insight and try not to be didactic
But to mark this merry moment let us try another tactic
A collection of scenes which at times may appear drastic
But be assured they're all procured from the realm of the fantastic

You may live in a semi detached with 2.3 sprogs
A steady routine and some family dogs
Or as digital nomads who populate blogs
Seeking out deep cuts to sell on discogs
Perhaps you'll obsess over collecting pogs
Or incline to the past time of snorkelling in bogs

Maybe you'll learn to play the sax from careless whispers
Or retire to your greenery to tend your aspidistras
Maybe you'll build monuments from the lolly sticks of twisters
Or become known in high circles as a pair of fashionistas

Perhaps you'll join a foreign feud romantic in resistance
And your image adorn t-shirts
Worn to rage against class systems
Then again you may start fretting
About suitable school catchments
Or foster mutual love of historic reenactments
In your spare time fashion trebuchets

From salvaged driftwood fragments

Maybe you'll pen odes on the transient
Nature of existential vagaries
Maybe you'll just be pleased you live near a big Sainsburys
Perhaps you'll espouse colloquies on medical oddities
Or champion the cause of downtrodden sororities

It could be none of the above will describe your priorities
And you'll live in a yurt assembling badly carved orreries
Feverishly plotting astronomical anomalies
To validate a growing faith in delusional homilies

Potentially you'll opt to renounce worldly possessions
And parade in penitence to atone for your transgressions
It could be as a double act you perfect risque impressions
And tour the comic circuit in the name of free expression
Till you sell a tell all memoir brimming with confessions
Before blithely settling down pursuing more sedate professions

On another note Perhaps you'll impart impacting lessons
On the cathartic possibilities of past life regression
Though I rather get the feeling and in this case it's a blessing
That such cases represent an unlikely digression

There's a chance you'll turn your studies onto egyptology
Become experts on Hatshepsut's hirsute semiology
Or perchance you'll dig on bugs and insect ecology
Become a power couple within entomology
With a focus on the locust and your own show on TV.

Perhaps you'll arrive at an interest in parquetry
Seek out rare trees in pursuit of floorboard artistry
You may try to channel Burroughs with some impromptu archery
I'd suggest that if you do aim away from any arteries

Irrespective of future paths yet to be travelled of yarns true and tall
That have not yet unravelled the corral of enjoyment a step made
Together expectantly stood to embark on whatever

But before you tire of these speculative embellishments of misery
And merriment
There's a level of replenishment intended with these sentiments in
Praise of all the elegance and erudite intelligence that makes of
You a pair who warrant all these celebrants,
Though you may face some impediments on the available
Evidence you've set an auspicious precedent and success
Appears as evident.

So all that remains is to simply wish you well
May you wend your way through life
Forging tales you wish to tell.

That Aint Half A Nice Shirt Brother

Now one evening Down the Albert
As we had a pre club brew
In the corner was a couple
Who had clearly had a few.
They duly approached our table
To engage in idle chatter
But what they really wanted
Well that was another matter.
To my mate they started talking,
Yes they'd taken quite a shine
And gregarious in nature
He gave freely of his time.
How'd you do? where you from?
And other such pleasantries
Shifted rather quickly
Once the couple felt at ease.

That aint half a nice shirt brother
With its most becoming cut
If I had that sort of clobber
Well I couldn't help but strut.
That aint half a nice shirt mister
Now the woman chimed in too
You must be fighting off the ladies
Can I be front of the queue

Such effusive observations
Grew more fulsome in their tone,
It sure brings out your eyes mate
This fine garment that you own.
That simple linen finish
And the neatly crafted stitch,
It ain't half a nice shirt brother,
Things continued at this pitch.

Whilst my friend remained
Chatty and oblivious
Their discursive advances
Seemed increasingly lascivious.
As they steered the conversation
In this suggestive direction
I wondered why they'd chosen
Such a source for their projection.
Not to disparage my associates
Sartorial selection,
But the raiment was quite plain
And did not deign
Such close inspection.

This exchange served to explain
Just how innocent my friend was.
Though amorously ardent
With proposed menage a trois
Application of their charms
Was not going to get them far.
Had he realised, the alarm
Would his demeanor surely mar

From such an invitation
He would himself have disbarred.
Being of a mindset
Quite conservatively trad
He'd be disinclined to find
Whether a good time could be had.

Yes, for my friend all such slight chances
Would only ever end in stasis.
And as for me, I guess I'd see
Take it on a case by case basis,
But this time I'd have declined
Because they both seemed kind of basic.

Crackpot Preachers

Crackpot preachers,
Over reachers,
False prophets,
And dodgy teachers.
Soap box heroes
Giving speeches,
Where from come
These crazy creatures?
All trying hard to beseech us
To renounce, rescind, repent
To all which I say, get bent.
Pluralism I'm all for
Yah weh, Allah, Vishnu, Thor
Gaia, Zeus, Krishna and more
All have their place in sacred lore.
That's all good, but I implore
In public, dull that zealous roar.
Sufi's, Jains, and pastafarians,
Jedi's, Buddhists, mad sectarians
Satanists and millenarians
Spiritualists, seminarians
And doubtless some other variants
Stake claims to enlightened ways.
I'm happy that you feel saved
Hallelujah, hip hip hooray.
But no I won't sign up today
No matter how much your display
Promises eternal rays

Of heavenly luminescence,
Inner wealth
And Divine presence.
If that's your path, good for you
May your beliefs see you through.
But if you feel moved to choose
That you must spread the good news
To demonstrate your piety,
Please do it fucking quietly.

Zizek's Sniff

Of contemporary noodle scratchers
There's a few kicking about
With varying degrees
Of insight nous and clout.
But for all the clever maxims
With which these thinkers riff
There's precious little matches up
To Slavoj Zizek's sniff.
His nasal punctuation
Pierces, pointed and precise,
When sometimes points are laboured
His proboscis sees him right.
As he dices twixt pop culture, Marx and
Good Old Jacques Lacan
It can seem convoluted
But his nostrils have a plan.

Others may scratch their beards,
Utilise upward inflection,
Drum their fingers, tug their ears
Or use sophist misdirection.
Some suggest cocaine usage
As the noisy nasal culprit
But the schnozzle leads the sermon
And the body's just the pulpit.
Adenoidal apertures the artist
And it's Slavoj that they've sculpted.
Like a Hegelian Pygmalion

His beak begets its creation
Dialectically inflecting
His materialist oration;
A reverse of the causation
In Gogol's imagination
Where the snout it once struck out
Now it leads the operation,
Not losing place upon the face
Where it can make its exhortations.
Ideologies are scrutinised
Imbued with novel meaning
Some tutored eyes say brutalised
Dependent on their leaning.
You may look down your nose
At the importance here suggested
Of quite how much the hooter
In the process is invested.
I would posit the hypothesis
Though it's not yet been means tested,
That his olfactory organ
Is not with snot congested
But the thoughts that are expressed
On all the notions he collected.
So go ahead if you wish
And this theory do refute
But I'm for the fragile absolute
Of his agile madcap snoot

Passing Wave

I would I were a passing wave
Then broken on the shore,
To me, to be that noble sea,
I could not ask for more.

Words For A

In Brugge, deluged with the news
That what I'd thought was just flu
Had been the final chapter for you.
Shocked fingers clasp a foreign brew

And try to construe the enormity of information received, just that
Instant bereaved.
A day follows of ghostlike wandering, dissociated and uncertain
Until back on home ground.

Many phone calls later and I'm informed by the sounds
Of professional, studiedly empathic phrasing
The terminological particulars of your terminal predicament.

Is that it?
In the final assessment the alien term arterio arterial sclerosis
Embeds itself indelibly in a lexicon previously devoid of such
Medical references.

I suppose this is the closest I can get to fathoming the biological
Process that culminates in the cessation of being.

There can be no further prognosis, or futile reconstitution of an
Ineluctable proposition. No pleading, no bargaining, no
Whataboutery exchanged with the definitive terms of the certain
Physician.

And yet it remained tinged with the hint of irreality initially.
Until the undeniable materiality of our final meeting, if that's the
Appropriate term for that fleeting and all too one sided greeting.

A strange endeavour attempting to converse with a cadaver.
I found I could only whisper, and briefly at that.

Even through the fug of disbelief and in all probability slight
Inebriety,
Having over utilised alcohol
To quell the groundswell
Of emotive overflow for a spell;
I knew I had to say something.

So that my battered grey matter
Coud reminisce about the dissemblance
Of the physical presence of the person
I used to get pissed with, play risk with,
Bought my first compact disc
And smoked my first spliff with.

Bringing me to thoughts of this,
Us freely exchanging big ideas but
Skirting around the crux of the issue with
All the intrepidity of inarticulate masculinity.
In spite of the fact that neither of us lacked
The necessary vocabulary to express ourselves with adequacy.

I now the sole orator, for lack of you as interlocutor.

An air of insouciance retrospectively seems affected, but perhaps
When all is now memory it's inevitably imperfectly reflected.

Our bantering back and forth
Indicative of some greater source
Of unspoken elements.
Secreted somewhere beneath the accreted sediment of inelegant
Posturing.
You denying your intelligence, me any propensity for sentiment.

Both disinclined to admit to anything as discernible as a softening
Of our mutually cynical positions on just about everything.

I looked at the plaque on the coffin bearing the inscription of your
Name and age.
Is that it?
A life reduced to finite digits a 5 and a 1
Or 160,833,600 seconds, give or take.

Or the cost of commemoration and subsequent incineration, about
4 months rent at Southwark council's current rate, or any number
Of bills left unpaid.

Do we take stock of a life in transactional terms, in the balance and
Measures of tangible treasures?
Hopefully not.

What remains in the impermanence of mortality that only looks
Blankly at the concept of eternal longevity
Through the promise of deities?
A fleeting instant of sorrow and jollity

Now moribund property.

No ever after shines beyond the conception of our limited minds.
So be it, perhaps all we have left is words.

I read avidly through the reams of ponderings and poetry you
Probably never thought I'd see.
Or possibly in some distant future
At a time of your preference
So you could provide censure or reference.

Your tortured musings, not meant for my perusing, but there wasn't
Really much chance of me choosing to not try to garner some
Meaning from them.

You were published once.
It cheered me to see a time when your words
Were less privately hoarded.

And what could I do but divine from those I'd found stored a guide
Of sorts of how to formulate thoughts on what we ought to do to
Say goodbye in a manner befitting your temperament.
More merriment and irreverence than stony faced remembrance.

I agonised about the editorial position I took in what would
constitute a posthumous edition of your written inscriptions.

A few excisions to render the final vision a lighter proposition than I
Initially encountered.
I renounced the doubts over which I had floundered.

Words are only ever received through second hand enunciation,
Even to ourselves in contemplation so why worry unduly.

I admit as now, agency, whilst I slightly sculpted them to the whims
Of my own intent, but I only did it to lighten the content a little.
You'd have understood I assume, the necessary small syntactic
Intrusion that allowed me to come to some form of conclusion:

That if our lives are a palimpsest endlessly drafted again,
I will write the next chapter as the ink has run dry in your pen.

www.ingramcontent.com/pod-product-compliance
Lightning Source LLC
LaVergne TN
LVHW020049110826
845155LV00029B/708

* 9 7 8 1 9 1 1 2 3 2 6 0 5 *